Good Night Las Vegas

An Illustrated Journey Through Iconic Landmarks, Vibrant Parks and Dazzling Attractions

Good Night Las Vegas

Title: Good Night Las Vegas
Series: Good Night Cities!

Cover design: LongTale Books

Published by: LongTale Books
Arlington, VA
http://longtalebooks.com

For information regarding permissions, please contact:
http://longtalebooks.com/contact

First Edition: 2023

Follow our story and art on instagram at https://www.instagram.com/longtalebooksco/

Connect with us on Twitter at https://twitter.com/longtalebooksco

Dedication

For the good-natured, spirited, and resilient people of Las Vegas - this book is dedicated to you. You are the soul that keeps the heartbeat of this vibrant city alive; your energy and love for life are what make Las Vegas truly magical. It is because of you that we can share with children not only the iconic landmarks but also hidden treasures of our beloved city. You embody hope, dreams, and endless possibilities - just like a child's innocent sense of wonder.

"Good Night Las Vegas" aims to evoke in young readers your admirable zest for life, curiosity to explore, and appreciation for diversity through an engaging journey within these pages.

Together, let us inspire them to dream big under starlit desert skies!

Introduction

"Discover the wonders of Las Vegas with 'Good Night Las Vegas,' a captivating story for our young explorers aged 1-5 years.

This enchanting journey through one of the world's most iconic cities is more than just a bedtime tale, it is an adventure that ignites imagination and nurtures curiosity. As we bid good morning, evening, and finally goodnight to intriguing landmarks, children will not only gain familiarity with the rhythmic flow of a day but also develop an appreciation for diverse cultures and experiences.

This lovingly crafted narrative is designed to be their first virtual tour guide to Las Vegas' spellbinding charm; from sparkling city lights to awe-inspiring natural wonders. So let's tuck them in as they dream about exploring vibrant landscapes under a starlit desert sky in this lively city!"

Good Night Las Vegas

Good morning, Las Vegas Strip! We're greeted by your dazzling lights and iconic landmarks.

Good Night Las Vegas

Good morning, Bellagio Fountains! Your magnificent water show mesmerizes us every time.

Good Night Las Vegas

Good morning, Fremont Street Experience! Your lively atmosphere and historic charm captivate us.

Good Night Las Vegas

Good morning, Red Rock Canyon! We're ready to explore your stunning natural beauty.

Good morning, High Roller Observation Wheel! We're excited to take in the panoramic view of the city.

Good Night Las Vegas

Good Night Las Vegas

Good morning, Neon Museum! Your vibrant displays tell tales of Vegas' colorful past.

Good Night Las Vegas

Good morning, The Venetian! Let's glide on a gondola down
your beautiful canals.

Good Night Las Vegas

Good Night Las Vegas

Good morning, Shark Reef Aquarium at Mandalay Bay! We're eager to meet the exotic marine life you protect.

Good Night Las Vegas

Good Night Las Vegas

Good morning, Springs Preserve! We're ready for another day of exploring your historic sites and botanic gardens.

Good Night Las Vegas

Good Night Las Vegas

Good evening, Caesar's Palace! The grandeur of your architecture always leaves us in awe.

Good evening, Adventuredome Theme Park! Thanks for a day filled with thrilling rides and laughter.

Good evening, Las Vegas Natural History Museum! We're fascinated by the stories of life on Earth you share.

Good Night Las Vegas

Good evening, Mount Charleston! We appreciate the tranquil break from the city bustle you provide.

Good Night Las Vegas

Good evening, Valley of Fire State Park! Your vibrant rock formations and desert vistas are a sight to behold.

Good Night Las Vegas

Good Night Las Vegas

Good evening, Flamingo Wildlife Habitat! Your tropical birds and creatures add an exotic touch to our evening.

Good Night Las Vegas

Good evening, Luxor Hotel! Your pyramid shape and Egyptian theme add a touch of mystery to our night.

Good Night Las Vegas

Good Night Las Vegas

About the Author

John Cole likes to write books with his children looking over his shoulder. His day job has always been as an engineer and entrepreneur, and writing gives him an opportunity to connect with his three kids. John can be found enjoying time with his family; his three children, three pet chickens, and 15,000 bees keep him busy.

Good Night Las Vegas

Good Night Las Vegas

Printed in Great Britain
by Amazon

29233104R00018